# #

YOUR TONGUE HAS THE POWER OF LIFE & DEATH

A 100 DAY DEVOTIONAL

LA'TICIA NICOLE

Purposely Created
PUBLISHING GROUP

#SpeakLife

Copyright © 2014 La'Ticia Nicole

All rights reserved. No part of this book may be reproduced, distributed or transmitted in any form by any means, graphics, electronics, or mechanical, including photocopy, recording, taping, or by any information storage or retrieval system, without permission in writing from the publisher except in the case of reprints in the context of reviews, quotes, or references.

Unless otherwise indicated, scripture quotations are from the New King James Version®. Copyright © 1982 by Thomas Nelson, Inc. All rights reserved.

Published by Purposely Created Publishing Group™

Printed in the United States of America

ISBN: 0-692-20774-0
ISBN-13: 978-0-692-20774-1

For more information, log onto
www.PurposelyCreatedPG.com

Dedication

✳

In Loving Memory of My Grandmother:
Inez Gant-Pitts
I will always love you!

Table of Contents

Acknowledgments..................................	xi
Introduction...	xiii
Why I #SpeakLife.................................	1

Section I
#SpeakLife into Your Health   3

Day 1...	4
Day 2...	6
Day 3...	8
Day 4...	10
Day 5...	12
Day 6...	14
Day 7...	16
Day 8...	18
Day 9...	20
Day 10...	22
Day 11...	24
Day 12...	26
Day 13...	28
Day 14...	30
Day 15...	32
Day 16...	34
Day 17...	36
Day 18...	38

Day 19	40
Day 20	42
Day 21	44
Day 22	46
Day 23	48
Day 24	50
Day 25	52

Section II
#SpeakLife into Your Finances	**55**
Day 26	56
Day 27	58
Day 28	60
Day 29	62
Day 30	64
Day 31	66
Day 32	68
Day 33	70
Day 34	72
Day 35	74
Day 36	76
Day 37	78
Day 38	80
Day 39	82
Day 40	84
Day 41	86
Day 42	88
Day 43	90

Day 44...	92
Day 45...	94
Day 46...	96
Day 47...	98
Day 48...	100
Day 49...	102
Day 50...	104

Section III
#SpeakLife into Your Relationships	107
Day 51..	108
Day 52..	110
Day 53..	112
Day 54..	114
Day 55..	116
Day 56..	118
Day 57..	120
Day 58..	122
Day 59..	124
Day 60..	126
Day 61..	128
Day 62..	130
Day 63..	132
Day 64..	134
Day 65..	136
Day 66..	138
Day 67..	140
Day 68..	142

Day 69………………………………………	144
Day 70………………………………………	146
Day 71………………………………………	148
Day 72………………………………………	150
Day 73………………………………………	152
Day 74………………………………………	154
Day 75………………………………………	156

Section IV
#SpeakLife into Your Career — 159

Day 76………………………………………	160
Day 77………………………………………	162
Day 78………………………………………	164
Day 79………………………………………	166
Day 80………………………………………	168
Day 81………………………………………	170
Day 82………………………………………	172
Day 83………………………………………	174
Day 84………………………………………	176
Day 85………………………………………	178
Day 86………………………………………	180
Day 87………………………………………	182
Day 88………………………………………	184
Day 89………………………………………	186
Day 90………………………………………	188
Day 91………………………………………	190
Day 92………………………………………	192
Day 93………………………………………	194

Day 94...	196
Day 95...	198
Day 96...	200
Day 97...	202
Day 98...	204
Day 99...	206
Day 100..	208

ABOUT THE AUTHOR	211

Acknowledgments

First and foremost, I would like to thank God who has always been the head of my life. You have been my protector, guidance, safety, help, inspiration, and all that I needed when in need!

To my grandmother, Inez Gant-Pitts and grandfather, Eddie Stanton – God said to teach a child in a way they should go and they won't waver. Both of my grandparents taught me the importance of family and keeping everyone together. I love and miss my grandparents very much. I pray I have made them proud. I'm trying.

To my mother, Nora Pitts – You were the first to introduce me to the Lord. I love you for being so strong. Watching you all my life taught me how never to give up on myself. Thank you, Mommy. I love you!

To my daddy, Gregory Stanton – Thank you for quiet strength. No one knows your story or would imagine what the Lord has done in our lives. I love you, Daddy!

To my husband, Antonio Beatty – Thank you for never trying to stop or hinder me from pursuing my purpose. I appreciate that very much.

To my two sons, Antonio Carlisle Beatty II and Aden Cole Beatty – You two are my #1 reason for going so hard. You're my reason for staying sane when Mommy want to fall to pieces at times. I look at your faces and pull myself together, and I keep pressing on. Mommy loves you!

To my family that keep pushing and believing in me: Uncle Jeffery Stanton, Aunt Lisa Stanton, Uncle Walter Pitts, Uncle Ronald Pitts, Uncle Jesse Pitts, and the late Uncle Johnny Pitts.

To Pastor Rose Thomas and my church family at Unfailing Love Christian Church – Thank you for believing in the God in me.

Thank you to all of my friends who always support my endeavors and push me into victory, no matter what. It's so many of you. I'm scared of missing names, so I will name the cities you live in: Detroit, Winston Salem, Charlotte, Durham, Dallas, and Atlanta.

I must send a special thank you to Tamica Jones, Shelley Moses, Vernice Gatland, Cher Taylor, Michele Simington Leverett, Amy Brooks, Bridget Rogers, Keya Jemmeh, Jeannie Martin, Ti Coger, Teresa Harris, Trina Holiness, Chandra Alston Southern, and Lakela Gillis.

Thank you to all the Professional Divas: Anissa Barbee, Tiffany Russel, Jennifer Pettiford, Kim Sessoms, Tiesha Powell, Lakenya Gibbs, Sharlease Collier, Denielle Vargave, Marice Beatty, and Shaundria and Torrence Williams.

Thank you to all of my friends and family, past radio show guests, listeners and social media followers. Without you, the vision wouldn't be able to go forth. Thank you for your love and support.

Special thanks to all of my trials and tribulations that birthed #SpeakLife. You didn't kill me. You made me stronger.

Introduction

A couples years ago, I decided to write a book about my life. I was at home alone with so much going through my mind that pain started to come over my body and cause my heart to hurt.

I thought about all the things that happened to me in my life that wasn't so good. It almost paralyzed me. I cried day and night. I went through this for months. Every time I wrote something painful, it pushed me back into the exact time that the painful events took place.

Then I realized that I hadn't healed from all the painful events. I then started to profess the goodness of God over my life. I started every morning by looking in the mirror and confessing the opposite of what I was feeling. I would tell myself I was happy when I was truly sad. I would tell myself I was rich when I didn't have money for bills. I would tell myself I was the head and not the tail while feeling like a failure.

I started to notice a change in my walk and in my stride. I started noticing that my life was lining up to the words that were coming out of my mouth. Each day it was getting easier to profess the goodness instead of seeing the bad. I started to focus on the good things that happened in my life as a result of the bad. That's when I knew that the devil was a defeated foe, and whatever he meant for bad, God would use for His good.

So, instead of my first book being about the bad things that happened to me, it ended up showing others *how to break free from negative thoughts.* If you can change your thoughts, you surely can change your life. I am a witness. Now I can write my life story without the pain and suffering. I can write my life story as a victor and not a victim.

To God be the Glory!

This book is for people that have negative thoughts and have a tendency of allowing those thoughts to paralyze them from their purpose. When you're able to heal from your past you'll be able to help someone else heal. I finally realized my testimony would help thousands to heal from wounds that they hid with bandages, but never took the bandages off to get air in order to heal properly.

When I feel the need to rejuvenate my mind, body and soul, I #SpeakLife and my faith in God reminds me that all things are possible.

La'Ticia

WHY I #SPEAKLIFE

From the time that I was five years old until I was ten, I was abused and molested by my babysitter. I carried the pain and shame with me until I realized that other women and children may have endured the same shattering experience. Upon learning how many women were affected by similar tragedies, I decided that it was time to reveal the truth and expose the devil.

In order to move forward, I realized that I had to change my surroundings. This change included my circle. I also changed the way I thought about mishaps and misfortune. I broke the bad habit of thinking I did something to bring it on myself when something bad happened, and realized that what doesn't kill me will make me stronger.

I refused to allow fear and shame to stop me from speaking the truth. Speaking about being molested and abused has broken chains for other families. In February 2013, I hosted an event called *Divas and Daughters*. You could see people being freed from bondage. As I spoke, I didn't blame anyone; I just spoke the truth. I told them even though these horrible things happened to me, it didn't justify or predict who I was going to be. It didn't make me a bad person. I am who God says I am: a virtuous woman, wife, mother, business owner, motivational speaker, Executive Director of a rehabilitation center, and so much more. What the devil meant for bad, God used for His good.

I founded Professional Divas with the primary mission to empower women. And as I speak the words "life" and "empowerment" to them, I am also speaking life and empowerment to myself.

※

For me, the beach is my refuge. While there, I like to reflect. When thinking of this period of drastic change, the lesson that I would like to share the most is this:

Learn to trust God and understand that "if God leads you to it, He will lead you through it." The past has led me to my purpose in life. My life has changed for the better, and I now know why I am on this journey.

Not everyone can emerge from child abuse and molestation, and somehow move forward in a positive way. But yet, I love with the love of the Lord and forgive like I want to be forgiven.

Each and every day I continue to #SpeakLife into myself. I challenge you to do the same for the next 100 days.

#SpeakLife
Into Your Health

✸

When you look in the mirror, what do you see?

I see a servant of God—a blessed, mighty woman. By actively and continually speaking these words, I grow into them. I am a blessed, mighty woman. I am perfectly imperfect. God used Peter, Martha, Mary, David, and so many others. Why not me?

I used to feel so unworthy of His love. Once, I asked flat out, "Lord who am I that you keep loving me and forgiving me and blessing me?"

He said, "You were made in my image, and I will never leave you, forsake you, nor see you beg for bread. You are my daughter and you are who I say you are. Eyes have not seen. Ears have not heard. Neither has it entered the hearts of men what I have for you. Have faith."

My response? "Okay!"

In order to manifest what God has for me, it's important to be the best me that I can be. Before you can love anyone else, you have to love yourself first. In order to effectively take care of and support someone else, you have to first take care of yourself. For this reason, I decided to dedicate the first 25 days of #SpeakLife into your health—mentally, emotionally, spiritually, and physically.

Day 1

Proverbs 15:13
A happy heart makes the face cheerful, but heartache crushes the spirit.

Proverbs 15:30
A cheerful look brings joy to the heart, and good news gives health to the bones.

✳

Reflection:
Make a positive difference in someone's life today. How? Smile. These are the only two verses in the bible that speak about smiling. I chose this to be my first topic in this devotional because this is the best thing you can give someone without saying a word. A happy heart makes a face cheerful, but heartache crushes the spirit. Smiling is contagious. When you smile, the world smiles back at you.

Goal:
I challenge you today to write down all the things that make you want to smile and see if it makes a difference in your day. I bet it will. Happy thoughts create a happy life!

#SpeakLife: Day 1

Day 2

Matthew 6:34
So do not worry about tomorrow; for tomorrow will care for itself. Each day has enough trouble of its own.

✳

Reflection:
Worrying is feeling uneasy, anxious, troubled, or distressed. It's a source of nagging concern. Something that bothers or disturbs our peace of mind. Worry can be caused by a person, thing, or situation (real or imagined) that we perceive as uncertain or potentially dangerous.

Goal:
Ask yourself: Why do I worry? What is it that causes me to worry?

Repeat after me:
I will not worry about the past, but I will plan for my future.

In Jesus' name, Amen!

Day 3

Proverbs 18:21
Death and life are in the power of the tongue, and those who love it will eat its fruits.

Reflection:
When you talk about your present circumstance what words are you using? Be mindful of what circumstances you bring to life with the words that you speak.

Goal:
Repeat after me:
I am blessed and rich.

I am delivered and set free from bondage.

I have the favor of God on my life.

I am a child of God and therefore have authority over the devil.

I have faith and won't throw in the towel when trouble comes.

I am more than a conqueror through Jesus Christ.

I #SpeakLife and fight with the armor of God.

What the devil meant for bad will work out for my good.

What I make happen for God, He will make happen for me.

I love with the love of the Lord.

I forgive like I want to be forgiven.

I have control over my tongue and body because I am disciplined.

In Jesus' name, Amen!

#SpeakLife: Day 3

Day 4

Mark 4:24
And He was saying to them, "Take care what you listen to. By your standard of measure it will be measured to you; and more will be given you besides."

✱

Reflection:
Remember you are what you eat. Make sure you're feeding your body and soul with the right food. While your body needs nutritional food, your soul needs prayer and positive words, so #SpeakLife.

Goal:
Write down what you're putting in your body, mind and soul. Is it positive?

What kind of music do you listen to?
What kind of books do you read?
Who is your mentor?

Evaluate the people in your circle. Are they positive?

#SpeakLife: Day 4

Day 5

1 Corinthians 15:33
Do not be misled: "Bad company corrupts good character."

※

Reflection:
Identify your life support. You are a giver. Connect with other givers and stop being used by users. If you're constantly giving, helping and promoting people that don't care about others, you're rewarding bad behavior. Stop it!

Goal:
Who have you accepted bad behavior from?
Can you change the way others treat you?
How are you going to change the way others treat you?

#SpeakLife: Day 5

DAY 6

PSALMS 23: 4
*Even though I walk through the darkest valley,
I will fear no evil, for you are with me; your rod and
your staff, they comfort me.*

REFLECTION:
When are you going to stop using sex, food, drugs, alcohol, people, gossip, places, etc. as pain medication? God is performing open heart surgery on you without anesthesia on purpose. Allow yourself to go through the surgery without pain relief. Pain guides you to your purpose. I am a witness.

GOAL:
How do you comfort yourself while walking through the darkest valleys? How does this medication make you feel?

If done in the presence of others, would it embarrass you? If so, then it's not right.

Write a letter to God, thanking Him and promising Him to make an honest effort to allow yourself to go through the surgery without the relief.

#SpeakLife: Day 6

Day 7

Mark 11:25
And whenever you stand praying, forgive; if you have anything against anyone, so that you're Father also who is in heaven may forgive you your trespasses.

※

Reflection:
Forgiveness gives you wings. When you let go of the weight you can fly higher. Who haven't you forgave from the past? How does unforgiving made you feel?
Have you ever done anything you had to apologize for? Did the person forgive you?

Goal:
Repeat after me:
I will love with the love of the Lord and forgive like I want to be forgiven.

#SpeakLife: Day 7

Day 8

Galatians 1:10
For am I now seeking the approval of man, or of God? Or, am I trying to please man? If I were still trying to please man, I would not be a servant of Christ.

❋

Reflection:
When will you learn that people pleasing won't get you anywhere? You can work your whole life trying to please people, but in the end, if you haven't fulfilled your purpose, you will feel extremely empty. Even with all your degrees and money if you're not living out your dreams you won't be happy. Don't try to please people. Walk towards your destiny which will lead to a purpose driven life.

#SpeakLife and #LiveOnPurpose

Goal:
Our purpose is discovered by way of our passions. While our passions lead us to our purpose, they also fuel and refresh our spirits when we find ourselves exhausted or confused. Make a list of your passions. Next to the ones that can be done alone, write the number one. Beside the ones that need a partner, write the number two.

Whenever you find yourself exhausted or confused, refer back to your list and act on your passions.

#SpeakLife: Day 8

Day 9

Jeremiah 32: 27
Behold, I am the Lord, the God of all flesh.
Is there anything too hard for Me?

※

Reflection:
God is in control. Not you! So go *sat down* somewhere! Yes, I said "sat." Oftentimes, particularly as "independent women," we have a tendency of wanting to be in control of every little detail in our lives. It's important that we know and trust that while we have a large say so over what goes on our lives, God has the ultimate say.

God not only carries you, but your family, your community, country, world, and galaxy. Trust that He knows what He is doing. He was running things before you, will do so after you, and if you have any intentions on living a full life, then it is critical that *you sat down*.

Goal:
Is there anything too hard for God? What area(s) of your life is too hard, or too much, for you to deal with right now?

Voice a sincere prayer, turning this burden over to the God of all flesh.

#SpeakLife: Day 9

Day 10

Genesis 1:27
So God created man in His own image; in the image of God He created him; male and female He created them.

Reflection:
You were made in His image. He went through hell, but look at Him now. The greater the challenge, the greater the victory. You were and are designed to be great. Believe it and receive it. Yes, I'm talking to you!

Goal:
Whenever you find yourself thinking negative thoughts or complaining, make this verbal exclamation: "I am great!"

#SpeakLife: Day 10

Day 11

2 Corinthians 4:13
Since we have the same spirit of faith according to what has been written, "I believed, and so I spoke," we also believe, and so we also speak.

✳

Reflection:
Give God the glory! He is so good! Speak things as though they aren't so they shall be! I am so excited about what God is doing in your life! He is a healer! He is your help in this present time of need!

Goal:
What do you need right now?

Really explore your emotional and physical needs and be honest. Do you need affection? Attention? Money? Healing?

Do you believe that God has already provided you with it? If so, write about one way that you can share your faith with someone else. If not, reflect on the why.

#SpeakLife: Day 11

Day 12

ECCLESIASTES 3: 1-8

To everything there is a season, and a time to every purpose under the heaven: A time to be born, and a time to die; a time to plant, and a time to pluck up that which is planted; A time to kill, and a time to heal; a time to break down, and a time to build up; A time to weep, and a time to laugh; a time to mourn, and a time to dance; A time to cast away stones, and a time to gather stones together; a time to embrace, and a time to refrain from embracing; A time to get, and a time to lose; a time to keep, and a time to cast away; A time to rend, and a time to sew; a time to keep silence, and a time to speak; A time to love, and a time to hate; a time of war, and a time of peace.

✳

REFLECTION:
Breaking News! We go through and we get through. *We just do.* It's called life. Thank God for it.

GOAL:
Have you ever gone through something that you thought would never end? Of course you have!

Reflect on this time. What happened?
Compare who you were before this experience and afterwards.

#SpeakLife: Day 12

Day 13

Proverbs 3: 5-6
Trust in the Lord with all your heart, and lean not on your own understanding; in all your ways acknowledge Him, And He shall direct your paths.

✽

Reflection:
Keep cool. God is working it out! Believe it!

Goal:
Reflect on a specific time when you leaned on God's understanding instead of your own. What was the outcome?

#SpeakLife: Day 13

Day 14

Psalm 121: 3
He will not let your foot slip —
He who watches over you will not slumber.

✽

Reflection:
Never underestimate God! He is working while you're sleeping.

Goal:
Now that you've been reminded that God works while you're asleep, share the message. Send an unexpected e-mail, text message, or card to someone, reminding them not to underestimate God.

#SpeakLife: Day 14

Day 15

PHILIPPIANS 2: 3-4

Do nothing from rivalry or conceit, but in humility count others more significant than yourselves.
Let each of you look not only to his own interests, but also to the interests of others.

REFLECTION:
#SpeakLife: You only have one life. Why not make it positive and expose the devil? You are who God says you are!

GOAL:
REPEAT AFTER ME:
I am blessed to be a blessing.

How are you a blessing to someone else?
Do you consider this is a blessing or a burden? Why?

#SpeakLife: Day 15

Day 16

Proverbs 17: 22
A joyful heart is good medicine, but a crushed spirit dries up the bones.

✴

Reflection:
Keep speaking positive over your life and I promise your body will line up. I am a witness. It's not easy, but it's worth it.

Goal:
How do you view your body?

Do you like it? Love it?

Hate it? Hate certain parts of it?

Write a love letter addressed to your body, giving it gratitude for supporting you to the best of its ability and make two vows to it. Be specific, and most importantly, be honest.

#SpeakLife: Day 16

Day 17

2 Corinthians 10: 3-5
For though we live in the world, we do not wage war as the world does. The weapons we fight with are not the weapons of the world. On the contrary, they have divine power to demolish strongholds. We demolish arguments and every pretension that sets itself up against the knowledge of God, and we take captive every thought to make it obedient to Christ.

✳

Reflection:
When the enemy comes in like a flood, you're going to have to lift up a standard. For example: You're being attacked by your family, friends, and foes. Opposition is coming from every direction. Don't fight back in the natural. You're going to have to pray and keep your mouth shut. Don't give ammunition to the fire. Keep calm and let the Lord fight your battles. Your blessing is on the way and the devil sees your victory coming. He is trying to keep your from it. Stay focused and keep your eyes on God.

Goal:
Do you have a "go-to" to resort to when the devil launches an attack? Is there a particular song that you like to sing? A dance? A prayer? Or, otherwise ritual? How does it work for you?

If you don't have one, explore such avenues that bring you joy and refreshes the love of God in your heart.

#SpeakLife: Day 17

Day 18

2 Corinthians 9:6
The point is this: whoever sows sparingly will also reap sparingly, and whoever sows bountifully will also reap bountifully.

✻

Reflection:
The words you put out in the atmosphere will not return to you void. Why not speak positive and change your life? For example, I tell my kids and myself that we can do all things through Christ who gives us strength. When you plant positive seeds, you get good fruit.

Goal:
It's easier to make something a habit if we do it at the same time and/or place. For example, whenever I pass a mirror, I tell myself that I am blessed. You could also remind yourself of your power through Christ every time you get into your car.

Make a list of five seeds that you can begin to sow every day.

#SpeakLife: Day 18

Day 19

Romans 12:12
*Rejoice in hope, be patient in tribulation,
be constant in prayer.*

※

Reflection:
Is patience something that you struggle with? Think of one way that you can strengthen your patience today whether it be at the red light, in the line at the grocer, dealing with a family member, or communicating with a co-worker. After all, impatience has a negative effect on your health.

Goal:
Repeat after me:
Lord, thank you for another day. I can't begin to tell you how much I appreciate your love, favor and grace. Lord, thank you for making us the head and not the tail, above and not beneath. We won't take our eyes off of you, Lord. Today will be another blessed day.

#SpeakLife: Day 19

Day 20

Jeremiah 33:6:
Behold, I will bring to it health and healing, and I will heal them and reveal to them abundance of prosperity and security.

Reflection:
God intended for you to be both healthy and wealthy. He said that He'd bring health and healing, revealing an abundance of prosperity and security. Never underestimate God! He is working while you're sleeping.

Goal:
What burden, stress, or illness do you need God to handle?

Who else in your life could benefit from an emotional and/or physical healing?

Pray for yourself and that person, making sure to quote today's scripture.

#SpeakLife: Day 20

Day 21

Philippians 4: 6-7
Do not be anxious about anything, but in everything by prayer and supplication with thanksgiving let your requests be made known to God. And the peace of God, which surpasses all understanding, will guard your hearts and your minds in Christ Jesus.

✳

Reflection:
Being anxious about something means that you're nervous about something that you believe could happen. It could also mean that you really want to do something. Don't put yourself in either category. Keep cool. God is working it out! Believe it!

Goal:
What are you anxious about?

What do you have a tendency to be anxious about?

Research the health consequence of anxiety. Is it worth it?

Pray that God will bless you with His peace, which surpasses all understanding.

#SpeakLife: Day 21

Day 22

John 10:10
The thief does not come except to steal, and to kill, and to destroy. I have come that they may have life, and that they may have it more abundantly.

✳

Reflection:
Do you have a Wait problem—not a weight problem, but a Wait problem? Stop waiting on people to justify who you are. You better know who you are. I am La'Ticia Nicole, a wife, a mother, a friend, a business owner, a fighter, and a woman of God. Who are you?

Goal:
What has the devil stolen (or is trying to steal) from you?

How will you get it back?

What are you waiting for?

Write about it.

#SpeakLife: Day 22

Day 23

1 John 4:18
There is no fear in love, but perfect love casts out fear. For fear has to do with punishment, and whoever fears has not been perfected in love.

※

Reflection:
You are worth loving. If you have to convince yourself that someone loves you, it's not love. They are filling a void that you have. Do yourself a favor and get whole before you add pain on top of pain.

Goal:
Whose love do you doubt?
Do you doubt someone else's love for you? Your love for them? Or, your love for yourself?

Is this doubt due to your own insecurities or due to their behavior?

Find a solution. Open the vessels of communication and talk about it. Bring God into the circle.

#SpeakLife: Day 23

Day 24

2 Corinthians 11:14
And no wonder, for even Satan disguises himself as an angel of light.

Reflection:
The devil is a dummy! A lion without teeth. Stop giving him power and dentures to bite you with. Heck, I'm talking to me, too! Love yourself unconditionally and continually #SpeakLife.

Goal:
What are habits of God?

What are habits of Satan?

Understand that Satan often disguises himself. However, by knowing his habits, you're more likely to see him coming from a mile away.

#SpeakLife: Day 24

Day 25

Colossians 1:16-17
For by him all things were created, in heaven and on earth, visible and invisible, whether thrones or dominions or rulers or authorities—all things were created through him and for him. And he is before all things, and in him all things hold together.

Reflection:
The world says you're ugly, fat, bald headed, skinny, and worth nothing. It says that you'll be just like your mama or daddy; you're a hoe, jobless, single, a cheater, etc. The list is endless. God says that you were made in His image. He said that you were created through Him and for Him. He said that you are more than a conqueror through His son, Jesus Christ. Who are you going to listen to?

Goal:
What have you been called by the world?

Which of these labels do you believe?

For every one of them, find a scripture that says otherwise.

Whenever you feel yourself falling back into the pit of self-pity, low self-esteem, or other bad habits, grab your scriptures.

#SpeakLife: Day 25

#SpeakLife into Your Finances

✳

Financial problems are many times generational problems. Your parents had little, their parents had little, and so on. Even if you have more, make sure that your mentality is in alignment with the Kingdom. Behaving rich does not mean unnecessarily splurging; this is also a "broke" mentality.

Kingdom thinking consists of tithing, saving, blessing others, and treating yourself kindly. If you could use a new coat, buy it! You deserve it! Don't skimp on yourself because you fear that the money won't be there tomorrow. If there is a class or conference that you would like to be a part of, go! Do it!

Our finances have much influence over our physical and emotional wellness. Therefore, it's of utmost importance that you #SpeakLife into your finances!

REPEAT AFTER ME:
I am rich and blessed.
I am alive and therefore worthy.
I am healthy and wealthy.
I have a purpose and I am great!

Day 26

1 Corinthians 10:13
No temptation has overtaken you except what is common to mankind. And God is faithful; he will not let you be tempted beyond what you can bear. But when you are tempted, he will also provide a way out so that you can endure it.

✳

Reflection:
God won't put more on you than you can handle.

Goal:
When it comes to money, what are your thoughts about it?

Do you believe it to be evil?

Do you associate it with drama?

Do you uphold the belief that it "comes and goes"?

Are you always in need of it?

Find three scriptures related to money and God's promises. Now, write a letter to money, combating your negative thoughts with the Word.

#SpeakLife: Day 26

Day 27

Matthew 5: 14-16

You are the light of the world. A city set on a hill cannot be hidden. Nor do people light a lamp and put it under a basket, but on a stand, and it gives light to all in the house. In the same way, let your light shine before others, so that they may see your good works and give glory to your Father who is in heaven.

✸

Reflection:

Take a moment to consider how powerful of a position it is to be the light of the world. While the world is in darkness, you are the light. You are the model, the example, and the way that it should be done. This is not to say that you won't make mistakes because you will. I'm only reminding you to be conscious of the words that you speak, particularly of those regarding your finances. After all, there's not much light in a lamp that is always "broke."

Goal:
Repeat after me:

Lord, I thank you for seeing something in me that you would use me. Take my hands, Lord and my feet. Touch my heart, Lord. Speak through me. If you can use anything, Lord, you can use me.

Thank you, Lord.

In Jesus' name, Amen!

#SpeakLife: Day 27

Day 28

Mark 11:22-23
"Have faith in God," Jesus answered. "Truly I tell you, if anyone says to this mountain, 'Go, throw yourself into the sea,' and does not doubt in their heart, but believes that what they say will happen, it will be done for them.

Reflection:
God's promises are made plain. He is dependable and will never let you down. Therefore, when approaching God, it's okay to have expectations. It's okay to expect miracles. Make sure that your request is in line with the Word.

Goal:
Repeat after me:
Lord, I love you. I place no one above you. Create in me a clean heart. I am asking for a fresh anointing, Father. On this day, I come to you with an attitude of faith and expectation. You told me to remind you of your word, Father, and believe in my heart that whatever I ask in the name of Jesus shall be done. I now see I can't do it alone, God.

I now see I need you in all areas of my life, Lord. I need you in my house. I need you in my finances. I need you at my job. I need you in my business. I need you in the courtroom. I need you while driving my car. I need you now, Lord! I need you now! And I'm expecting a miracle. Amen!

#SpeakLife: Day 28

Day 29

Matthew 6:34
So do not worry about tomorrow; for tomorrow will care for itself. Each day has enough trouble of its own.

Reflection:
Worry is feeling uneasy, anxious, troubled, or distressed. A source of nagging concern. Something that bothers or disturbs our peace of mind. Worry can be caused by a person, thing, or situation (real or imagined). Something we perceive as uncertain or potentially dangerous. I speak so much on worrying because it's a common problem. Its results are strictly negative.

Goal:
Answer the following questions:

1. Why do I worry?
2. What is it that causes me to worry?
3. In my own words, what is worry?

Afterwards, Repeat after me:
I will not worry about the past, but I will plan for my future.

In Jesus' name, Amen!

#SpeakLife: Day 29

Day 30

Matthew 7:7
Ask and it will be given to you; seek and you will find; knock and the door will be opened to you.

Reflection:
Have you ever been in desperate need of a financial breakthrough, and just when you began to think there was no way out, it showed up? Didn't it feel like the atmosphere changed? All good things will give you this amazing feeling. Make yourself comfortable with it.

Goal:
Stop worrying about things you can't change. Speak into your family life. Speak things as though they shall be. Make God the head of your life and put the small things behind you.

Prayer changes things. Pray until you enter heaven. You will feel the atmosphere change.

#SpeakLife: Day 30

Day 31

Proverbs 31: 29-31
"Many daughters have done well, But you excel them all."
Charm is deceitful and beauty is passing,
But a woman who fears the Lord, she shall be praised.
Give her of the fruit of her hands,
And let her own works praise her in the gates.

※

Reflections:
Proverbs 31 is by far one of my favorite verses in the bible. Every time I read it, I find a gem that I'd previously overlooked. Oftentimes it helps to break chapters down into verses. Instead of studying the entire chapter, meditate on a few verses of it. There, you'll find treasure.

Goal:
Repeat after me:
I am the virtuous woman mentioned in Proverbs 31.
I #SpeakLife into dead situations.
Greater He that is in me than He that is in the world.
I have control over my tongue and my body.
I bind envy and rebuke strife.
I have peace and joy.
I am rich. So rich that money runs after me; I don't have to chase it.
I am delivered and set free from sin and bondage.
Therefore, I stay away from drama.
God is my healer, my deliverer, my keeper, and my wheel.

In Jesus' name, Amen!

#SpeakLife: Day 31

Day 32

Matthew 7: 24-27

"Everyone then who hears these words of mine and does them will be like a wise man who built his house on the rock. And the rain fell, and the floods came, and the winds blew and beat on that house, but it did not fall, because it had been founded on the rock. And everyone who hears these words of mine and does not do them will be like a foolish man who built his house on the sand. And the rain fell, and the floods came, and the winds blew and beat against that house, and it fell, and great was the fall of it."

※

Reflection:
Your come up could be your set up. Make sure you're building on a solid foundation.

Goal:
Sometimes in the hustle and bustle of trying to make a living for ourselves, we lose sight of our foundation.

What does your foundation consist of?

If possible, conduct this conversation with your family.

Day 33

1 Thessalonians 5:18:
Give thanks in all circumstances; for this is the will of God in Christ Jesus for you.

✳

Reflection:
Sometimes you just need to say thank you. As your #SpeakLife advocate, even I sometimes have difficulty finding something positive to say. Life has a way of doing this to us. When you find yourself in such predicaments, tell Him thanks. When you don't know what else to say, tell Him thanks.

Goal:
Repeat this at least ten times today:

"Lord, I thank you for making a way out of no way."

Day 34

Hebrews 13:8:
Jesus Christ is the same yesterday and today and forever.

※

Reflection:
God doesn't change. He can't. We do. Not only do we change, but it's important that we do. Furthermore, if you want a change, then you must make up your mind to change your situation.

Think it! Believe it! Say it! Do it! *In that order.*

Goal:
How would you like to change your financial situation?

Identify three changes—physically and mentally—that you must make in order to turn your financial situation around.

#SpeakLife: Day 34

Day 35

Philippians 4:19:
And my God will supply every need of yours according to his riches in glory in Christ Jesus

---

Reflection:
Sometimes you have to experience a loss to see how big your God is. Your faith has to be stretched. When you thought you lost that job; God was your provider. When you lost your parent(s); God was your parent. When all your hope was gone and you couldn't take one more thing; God was your keeper. When all the bill collectors kept calling and your bank account was at zero; God was your provider. When that man/woman tried to beat the life out of you; God was your protector. When your family/friends forsake you; God said He will never leave you, forsake you, nor see you begging for bread.

Goal:
If God did it once, he will do it again!

Reflect on a few times that God really came through as your provider.

Now, thank Him for it. Get emotional with it!

#SpeakLife: Day 35

Day 36

LUKE 18:27
He replied, "What is impossible for people is possible with God."

※

REFLECTION:
God uses the unlikely to do the impossible. I am a witness. I have seen him do it. He provides for me and makes ways out of no way. When I moved to North Carolina in 1992, I had fifteen dollars to my name. I had no choice but to take it one day at a time because I had no clue how I was going to make it. If He did it for me, He'll do it for you. That's why I speak life.

GOAL:
Does being debt free seem like an impossible task? Breathe this scripture into your circumstance.

"What is impossible for people is possible with God." You will be debt free!

#SpeakLife: Day 36

Day 37

Ephesians 4: 26-27
"Be angry, and do not sin": do not let the sun go down on your wrath, nor give place to the devil.

Reflection:
As you can see, I am not allowing the devil to shut me up! Open your mouth and #SpeakLife. Hasn't he stolen enough from you? Maybe it's just me, but I work hard for the stuff I had that he took from me. I want my blessings!

Goal:
One sure way of giving place to the devil is speaking ill of your situation. The good news is that it's not too late to turn it around.

Tell the devil to take his dirty paws off your stuff and give it back!

#SpeakLife: Day 37

Day 38

Matthew 6: 31, 32
Therefore do not be anxious, saying, 'What shall we eat?' or 'What shall we drink?' or 'What shall we wear?' For the Gentiles seek after all these things, and your heavenly Father knows that you need them all.

Reflection:
The Lord keeps making a way out of no way. You may not be perfect. You may not have diamonds and riches, but what you have is the favor of God upon your life and that is so much more than tangible things.

Goal:
Verbally declare right now that you'll stop worrying about financial needs. Instead, you'll trust God's Word that He knows what we need and will provide them all.

#SpeakLife: Day 38

Day 39

Deuteronomy 28: 1, 2
"Now it shall come to pass, if you diligently obey the voice of the Lord your God, to observe carefully all His commandments which I command you today, that the Lord your God will set you high above all nations of the earth. And all these blessings shall come upon you and overtake you, because you obey the voice of the Lord your God.

※

Reflection:
The Word has been spoken. All you have to do is obey the voice of God. Do you believe that? You can make a positive change at this very second if you get out your own way. *Selah*

Goal:
In what way(s), are *you* in your own way? Perhaps you're operating from a place of lack, believing that you don't have enough of this or that to do what needs to be done.

#SpeakLife: Day 39

Day 40

1 Corinthian 9: 24
*Do you not know that those who run in a race all run,
but one receives the prize?
Run in such a way that you may obtain it.*

Reflection:
Stop fighting against yourself. You are who you think you are. If you think you're a loser, you are! Speak life into yourself. Don't wait on others to justify who you are. Stop acting defeated and fight!

Goal:
Look into the mirror and tell yourself, "I am a winner. I am blessed, healthy, and wealthy."

#SpeakLife: Day 40

Day 41

Matthew 19:24
Again I tell you, it is easier for a camel to go through the eye of a needle than for a rich person to enter the kingdom of God.

Reflection:
He didn't say that it was impossible. He only said that it wasn't easy. No one would like to think that money would change them. However, if that were so, this scripture would not exist.

Goal:
Identify five ways that you intend to stay grounded once your bank account reflects your wealth.

#SpeakLife: Day 41

Day 42

Deuteronomy 8:18
You shall remember the Lord your God, for it is he who gives you power to get wealth, that he may confirm his covenant that he swore to your fathers, as it is this day.

※

Reflection
God intended for you to be wealthy. In fact, He promised your forefathers that you would have wealth. Make sure that your thoughts and behaviors line up with God's intentions.

Goal:
Answer the following questions:
1. How do you plan to obtain wealth?

2. How do your plans reflect your love of God?

3. How do you plan to maintain your wealth once you have it?

#SpeakLife: Day 42

Day 43

Malachi 3:10

Bring the full tithe into the storehouse, that there may be food in my house. And thereby put me to the test, says the Lord of hosts, if I will not open the windows of heaven for you and pour down for you a blessing until there is no more need.

❋

Reflection:
God didn't say that a percentage of your tithes would lead to an outpour of blessings. He said to bring full tithe into the storehouse.

Goal:
Repeat after me:
Hear my cries!

Bless everyone around me, Lord.

Prepare our minds and hearts for the next time that you open the windows of heaven.

Bless me so that I can bless others.

Walk with me daily.

In Jesus' name, Amen!

#SpeakLife: Day 43

Day 44

Matthew 11:28-30
Come to me, all who labor and are heavy laden, and I will give you rest. Take my yoke upon you, and learn from me, for I am gentle and lowly in heart, and you will find rest for your souls. For my yoke is easy, and my burden is light.

✶

Reflection:
If your spirit is heavy and you have unresolved issues, take it to God in Prayer. He is waiting on you to turn to Him. Stop holding hurt, pain, unforgiveness, the past, rejection, rape, lies, abandonment, and abuse. Free yourself from those burdens!

Goal:
Repeat after me:
I am not a victim. I am victorious.

In Jesus' name, Amen!

#SpeakLife: Day 44

Day 45

Matthew 6:14
For if you forgive others their trespasses, your heavenly Father will also forgive you (Attitude: forgive because you love the Lord).

Reflection:
What does this mean to you? If someone owes you a debt, do you have a right to be upset with them? Yes! You do. However, acknowledge your feelings and let it go. Continuing to hold on to a grudge over money is the same as believing that your blessings are limited. They are not. Forgive them and move on.

Goal:
Repeat after me:
I will love with the love of the Lord and forgive like I want to be forgiven.

#SpeakLife: Day 45

Day 46

Proverbs 18:21
Death and life are in the power of the tongue, and those who love it will eat its fruits.

Reflection:
When you talk about your present circumstance what words are you using? Make sure that they reflect the Word of God. Remember, you are the light of the world.

Goal:
Repeat after me:
I am blessed, rich, delivered, and set free from bondage.

I have the favor of God on my life.

I am a child of God and therefore have authority over Satan.

I have faith and can stand firm when trouble comes.

I am more than a conqueror through Jesus Christ.

I #SpeakLife.

I am disciplined and continually practice having control over my tongue.

In Jesus' name, Amen!

#SpeakLife: Day 46

Day 47

Luke 7:47

"…Therefore I tell you, her sins, which are many, are forgiven—for she loved much. But he, who is forgiven little, loves little." And he said to her, "Your sins are forgiven."

✲

Reflection:
If God can forgive us, surely we can forgive each other and ourselves. One reason that debt is an ongoing problem for many of us is because we failed to forgive ourselves for obtaining so much debt in the first place.

Goal:
Repeat after me:
I will love myself with the love of God and forgive myself just as God has already forgiven me. My choices from this day forward will reflect this love and compassion.

In Jesus' name, Amen!

#SpeakLife: Day 47

DAY 48

LUKE 6:38
Give, and it will be given to you. Good measure, pressed down, shaken together, running over, will be put into your lap. For with the measure you use it will be measured back to you.

※

REFLECTION:
There is an unspeakable joy in being able to give. However, having been taken advantage of for a period of time can leave you drained. Don't allow it to. You are not bitter. You are better! Plus, today's scripture demonstrates the result of having a generous spirit.

GOAL:
Take a look at your budget and determine how much you can afford to give. Even if it's just one dollar bill; that's something.

Now, find an organization that makes your heart flutter. If kids are your passion, look into that. If it's the elderly, pets, or abused persons, look there.

Commit to giving what you can afford over a period of time.

#SpeakLife: Day 48

Day 49

Luke 14:28
For which of you, desiring to build a tower, does not first sit down and count the cost, whether he has enough to complete it?

Reflection:
You have a desire. Prior to making the purchase, it's important that you "first sit down and count the cost." Can you afford it? Today, everything is capable of being financed. Just because you are approved for the loan does not necessarily mean that you can afford it.

Goal:
How can you be trusted with a lot if you cannot be trusted with little?

Go over your budget. If you don't already have one, then this is the perfect opportunity to create one.

Separate the needs from the wants.

Now, study the wants and determine if you can afford them.

#SpeakLife: Day 49

Day 50

Proverbs 13:7
One pretends to be rich, yet has nothing; another pretends to be poor, yet has great wealth.

Reflection:
Today, we call this "fronting," "faking the funk," "hood rich," "ghetto fabulous," and a slew of other terms. Don't fall into this category. Don't even fake it until you make it. Instead, faith it until you make it. Act your wage!

Goal:
Are you acting your wage?

Are you setting aside something to save prior to splurging?

If not, what are some changes that you can make in order to do so?

If you already are, then share today's scripture. You never know who may be blessed by it.

#SpeakLife: Day 50

#SpeakLife into Your Relationships

✳

Please know that God loves you! When we as people feel unloved we search for forms of love. We end up giving ourselves away to fulfill the emptiness. Before you know it, your name is everywhere. You have fooled yourself into falling in love with people that are not even ready for relationships, let alone marriage. You end up full of hurt.

Allow God to love on you. Let him be your hiding place until you know he loves you. Then you'll know what love feels like. When you're crying and feeling alone you'll feel him as a comforter. He loves you so much, that he gave his only son for your sins. God said that He will supply all your needs according to his riches and glory. Believe him! Trust him! *Oh, taste and see that the Lord is good.*

I'm praying for peace that passes understanding for you. I'm praying for your joy. I'm praying for your marriage—whether you're already married, soon to be, or praying to be. You must learn to be married to Him first. I'm praying for the bond that you share with your siblings, other family members, and especially the one with the children in your life. For the relationships that exist on your job, in your business, at the church, in your neighborhood, and the ones that are soon to come.

Not my will, Lord.

But your will be done.

In Jesus' name, Amen!

Day 51

Psalms 139: 13-15
For you formed my inward parts; you knitted me together in my mother's womb. I praise you, for I am fearfully and wonderfully made. Wonderful are your works; my soul knows it very well. My frame was not hidden from you, when I was being made in secret, intricately woven in the depths of the earth.

※

Reflection:
You are worth loving! No matter what. Don't allow the enemy to trick you to believe you're unlovable. Your past is your past. You are a beautiful sculpture of your ugly past. Now walk with your head up high and know that your mistakes are now your message.

Goal:
Write a letter to the little girl inside of you. For the sake of this mission, we'll say that she is six years old. Who is she compared to who you are now?

What beautiful, uninhibited parts of her crouched itself in a corner due the tragedies of life? What advice would give her? What advice can she give you?

This exercise will help to rebuild this essential relationship with the little girl inside of you.

#SpeakLife: Day 51

Day 52

2 Timothy 2: 23-25
Have nothing to do with foolish, ignorant controversies; you know that they breed quarrels. And the Lord's servant must not be quarrelsome but kind to everyone, able to teach, patiently enduring evil, correcting his opponents with gentleness. God may perhaps grant them repentance leading to a knowledge of the truth.

✹

Reflection:
Watch out for strife, and stay away from people that bring it. It's a trick to make you regress to the old you. The devil only comes to kill, steal, and destroy.

Goal:
Pop culture seems to reinforce strife within our social communities. We see and crave for it in reality shows. Many of the books that we read are centered on drama. Oftentimes there is strife within our families, our churches, and our workplaces as well.

Identify all the ways that you are surrounded by conflict.

How do you react to it?

Is this in alignment with how God wants you to act? If not, then how can you realign your behavior?

#SpeakLife: Day 52

Day 53

1 Corinthians 2:13
This is what we speak, not in words taught by human wisdom but in words taught by the Spirit, expressing spiritual truths in spiritual words.

Reflection:
#SpeakLife is not just words. Like love, it's a verb; it's action.

Goal:
Knowing that you are not just talking, but are making spiritual mountains move, open your mouth and REPEAT AFTER ME:

My family and I are healthy.
My children are safe from hurt, harm or danger.
I am rich, blessed, and debt free.
I bind strife, confusion, and envy.
I rebuke generational curses.
I release a spirit of peace because I have joy.

I love others in spite of their downfalls, understanding that no one is perfect but God.

I will not procrastinate on my goals.
I do not have the spirit of fear, but of a sound mind.
I do not make assumptions; I am a thinker.
No weapon formed against me shall prosper; I believe God.

#SpeakLife: Day 53

Day 54

Ephesians 4:29
Let no corrupting talk come out of your mouths, but only such as is good for building up, as fits the occasion, that it may give grace to those who hear.

✳

Reflection:
Stop telling people how bad others are and show them how good of a person you can be. Downing others will not make your situation look better. Remember the same people you meet on the way up, you see them on the way down.

Goal:
It's so easy to get wrapped up in gossip. That's because it's easier to shake our heads at another's falls rather than shine the light on our own.

Make a conscious effort today to avoid both speaking and entertaining gossip.

Allow today's scripture to meditate on your heart and whenever you feel tempted, reflect on it.

#SpeakLife: Day 54

DAY 55

1 CORINTHIANS 13: 11

When I was a child, I spoke like a child, I thought like a child, I reasoned like a child. When I became a man, I gave up childish ways.

REFLECTION:

Growing older is inevitable but growing up is a choice. On the topic of immaturity, we are quick to think of the childish person(s) we know. Instead, ponder on the relationship that you have with God. How much stronger is your faith than it was last year? Three years ago? A decade ago?

GOAL:

Identify three activities that you can do within the next three months to strengthen your relationship with God.

You are no longer a child. Therefore, you should no longer speak, think, pray, and behave like a child.

Boldly step into the heels of the virtuous woman that God intended you to be.

#SpeakLife: Day 55

Day 56

Proverbs 14:30
A tranquil heart gives life to the flesh, but envy makes the bones rot.

✳

Reflection:
People shouldn't be jealous of others' harvest. You don't know how long they've been planting and laboring for their fruit. Furthermore, envy stirs not necessarily because we want the physical thing that another person has, but because we believe that if we had that thing, then we would also have what we perceive that the thing will bring along with it. For example, it's easy to believe that another woman's good looks will allow her a better selection of mates. That a luxury car or big house means that money is not issue. Envy is a waste of time and energy.

Goal:
We all have desires and there will always be someone else out there who already possesses it. Jealousy is a natural reaction of the flesh.

It's important to equip your spirit with the necessary tools to combat the flesh.

Find two other verses on jealousy and recite them aloud.

#SpeakLife: Day 56

Day 57

1 Peter 5:8
Be sober-minded; be watchful.
Your adversary the devil prowls around like a roaring lion,
seeking someone to devour.

✻

REFLECTION:
Sometimes God has you by yourself to protect you! Allow him! Stop chasing after people that don't have your best interest at heart. While you're praying for them, they're somewhere *preying* on you. Allow God to remove those people! He is trying to take you somewhere, but you have too much weight on you. Rejection is protection!

GOAL:
Verbally thank God for the romance that didn't last, for the job that you didn't get, for the friend that didn't show up, etc.

The next time you're rejected, instead of looking inward, smile and look upward. It was God protecting you.

#SpeakLife: Day 57

Day 58

Psalm 85:10
Steadfast love and faithfulness meet; righteousness and peace kiss each other.

※

Reflection:
We all have sinned and come short of His glory. Stop acting fake and tell the whole story. Then, and only then, will God get the glory.

Goal:
Dissect today's scripture. You may know the definition of each word, but look them up anyway. For instance, we all know that righteousness means doing right, but did you know that it also means being genuine?

Being genuine means keeping it real, telling the whole story.

Break it down into laymen's terms and read it again with a new understanding.

#SpeakLife: Day 58

Day 59

John 10:10
The thief comes not, but to steal, and to kill, and to destroy: I am come that they might have life, and that they might have it more abundantly.

Reflection:
Stop allowing others to whore your spirit. When you find that someone comes around to take and never deposit anything, you might be around a spirit robber. When you find that when you're around those type of people, you feel weak after they leave, you might be around a spirit robber. When you feel like they secretly talk bad behind your back, but they support you in your face, you just might have a spirit robber in your midst. These types of people are led by envy and strife. They're secretly jealous of your blessings that you may take for granted. Ask God to show you your spirit robber. Then remove them from your circle. They will try to suck the life out of your friendship for their own personal gain.

Goal:
As women we were blessed with something called an intuition. It's our internal GPS given to us by God. Our intuition will allow us to spot trouble before it comes. Before a person opens their mouth, we'll know what their intentions are. It's important to keep your intuition alert and nourished; do this by listening to it. Identify ways that you can strengthen your intuition. This is also a great exercise to do with your girlfriend(s).

#SpeakLife: Day 59

Day 60

Proverbs 15:4
A gentle tongue is a tree of life, but perverseness in it breaks the spirit.

Reflection:
Start your morning with positive words over your children and yourself. Tell your children that they are smart, loved, good, special, wonderful, protected, valued, handsome, pretty, healthy, wealthy, and the most beautiful gift given to you.

Goal:
Repeat after me:
I am blessed.
I am valued.
I am healthy.
I am rich.
I have control over my mouth.
I have control my body.
I love the Lord and He loves me.
I have the favor of God on my life.
My family is blessed.

In Jesus' name, Amen!

#SpeakLife: Day 60

Day 61

Matthew 11: 28-30
Come to me, all who labor and are heavy laden, and I will give you rest. Take my yoke upon you, and learn from me, for I am gentle and lowly in heart, and you will find rest for your souls. For my yoke is easy, and my burden is light.

Reflection:
Your tree is heavy because you have too many dead branches on it. Cut them off so that your fruit can grow!

Goal:
Cutting off dead branches doesn't always mean removing the person from your life. It also means acknowledging the burden, finding a solution, and opening the airways of communication. Sometimes our "dead branches" don't even know that they're burdens. And unless you bring it to their attention, they won't know.

Who are some of the dead branches in your life?

Do they know?

What solution would best remedy the situation?

#SpeakLife: Day 61

Day 62

Proverbs 13:20
Whoever walks with the wise becomes wise, but the companion of fools will suffer harm.

Reflection:
Never be fooled. Bad company corrupts good manners. If you plan on going places, why hang out with someone who doesn't ever leave the darn house?

Goal:
Repeat after me:
I will attract the kind of friends that will complement the person God wants me to be.

Now, look in the mirror and #SpeakLife.

#SpeakLife: Day 62

Day 63

1 Peter 3:1
Wives, in the same way submit yourselves to your own husbands so that, if any of them do not believe the word, they may be won over without words by the behavior of their wives.

※

Reflection:
Speak over your relationships. If you're not married yet or are divorced, start speaking life into yourself and ask God for the kind of traits you want in a spouse. Be specific. If you are, then not only should you #SpeakLife to your children. #SpeakLife to your spouse as well. This will strengthen your marriage. Who wouldn't want a man or a woman of God who cherishes the relationship?

Goal:
Repeat after me:
We have each other because we love each other.
We are faithful and protect one another.

My husband loves his wife as Christ loves the church.
My wife submits to me and loves me.

We communicate effectively and do our best to take care of each other's needs.

No devil in hell can split us up; what God put together, *no man* will put us under.

In Jesus' name, Amen!

#SpeakLife: Day 63

Day 64

John 3:16
For God so loved the world that he gave his one and only Son

REFLECTION:
God made a sacrifice because He loves us. So we can put down our pride, shame, grudges, strife, hurts and anger to show love. Don't forget to pray over your family before they leave out the door. Family is so important and precious. The devil is out to kill, steal and destroy the family.

I have learned from my pastor to tell the devil *Hell no!* You can't have my family. I will text and call those that don't want to talk. I will love on people that have in their mind that no one loves them. I will keep peace and show love. We must lead by example.

GOAL:
REPEAT AFTER ME:
I love with the love of the Lord and forgive like I want to be forgiven.

Day 65

Romans 12:2
Do not be conformed to this world, but be transformed by the renewal of your mind, that by testing you may discern what is the will of God, what is good and acceptable and perfect.

Reflection:
When you're striving for success not everyone is going to be praying for you, some may prey on you. Learn the difference and keep speaking life to yourself. You're changing and it's not for people to understand. You're being purged and everything and everybody that's being burned off is necessary. Purging hurts, but I promise you will come out like a shiny diamond.

Goal:
Transformation by renewal is a continual process. When it is not, then we need to check ourselves. Perhaps our speech, thoughts, behavior, or company does not reflect the renewal that we seek.

Are you in the process of transformation? If not, consider why; find the bad root. Then, make a list of five ways that you can recognize when you're off course, and another five ways that you reconnect with God.

#SpeakLife: Day 65

Day 66

Proverbs 22: 6
Train up a child in the way he should go; even when he is old, he will not depart from it.

※

Reflection:
Don't forget to #SpeakLife to your children. Plant the seed early and watch it grow.

Goal:
How would it have benefited you to hear, on a consistent basis, that you were beautiful, smart, loved, a prized possession, destined to be great, etc.?

Plant these seeds into the children in your life.

Reach out to a child today and plant a positive seed.

#SpeakLife: Day 66

Day 67

Matthew 11:28
Come to me, all who labor and are heavy laden, and I will give you rest

Psalm 51:10:
Create in me a clean heart, O God, and renew a right spirit within me.

✳

Reflection:
Don't allow a hard heart to steal your victory. You can't hold hatred and unforgiveness and think you're going to live a happy life. Let go of your hatred for the parent that did you so wrong. Let go of the people that broke your heart. Let go of the friends that turned into foes. Let go of your rapists and abusers. Let *them* go, so *you* can live.

Goal:
Reflect on who hurt you.

Can you forgive them?

Can you forgive yourself?

Why must you forgive?

#SpeakLife: Day 67

Day 68

James 4:7
Therefore submit to God. Resist the devil and he will flee from you.

❋

Reflection:
You're being tested because the devil sees your promise. Fight with your faith!

Goal:
What are you going through?

What area of your life is…uncomfortable?

Is the tension in your love life?

A battle with low self-esteem or depression? On the job?

If this problem did not exist, how much better would your life be?

What does submitting to God in this situation mean to you?

In what ways (physical or mental) are you surrendering to Satan?

#SpeakLife: Day 68

Day 69

Galatians 3:10
For all who rely on works of the law are under a curse; for it is written, "Cursed be everyone who does not abide by all things written in the Book of the Law, and do them."

※

Reflection:
Every morning you wake up, you must prepare yourself to deal with relationships—with yourself, God, family, friends, business partners, etc. Therefore, it's important to #SpeakLife over your day prior to getting out bed. Ready?

Goal:
Repeat after me:
Today is a great day. I have joy and peace.
I am blessed and healthy. I am wealthy and wise.
I'm not what or who I used to be.
My steps are ordered by the most hight God.

My family is blessed and all generational curses are broken now!

Friends and family relationships are being repaired now!

I am the head and not the tail; I am above and not beneath.

I am a positive person because I have favor.

In Jesus' name, Amen!

#SpeakLife: Day 69

Day 70

Isaiah 54:17
No weapon that is formed against thee shall prosper; and every tongue that shall rise against thee in judgment thou shalt condemn. This is the heritage of the servants of the LORD, and their righteousness is of me, saith the LORD.

※

REFLECTION:
The devil is trying to shut you up. Understand why he tries to fight you so hard. *You have generations inside of you.* If he can get you to believe that all hope is gone, he has won against many, not just you.

GOAL:
REPEAT AFTER ME:
I am delivered and set free from bondage.
I have the favor of God on my life; therefore, I #SpeakLife.

I am a child of God and thereby have authority over the devil.

I have faith and I won't throw in the towel when trouble comes.

I fight with the armor of God.
I am more than a conqueror through Jesus Christ.

What the devil meant for bad will work out for my good.

I have faith. No weapons formed against us shall prosper.
In Jesus' name, Amen!

#SpeakLife: Day 70

Day 71

Luke 10: 16-20
"Whoever listens to you listens to me; whoever rejects you rejects me; but whoever rejects me rejects him who sent me." The seventy-two returned with joy and said, "Lord, even the demons submit to us in your name." He replied, "I saw Satan fall like lightning from heaven. I have given you authority to trample on snakes and scorpions and to overcome all the power of the enemy; nothing will harm you. However, do not rejoice that the spirits submit to you, but rejoice that your names are written in heaven."

✻

Reflection:
Why in the world would you let another sinner saved by grace, remind you of your past mistakes? Come on now, really? I need you to know who you are. You went through. You've gone through. They did too! So, what?

Goal:
Repeat after me:
I am more than a conqueror through Jesus.
I am a new person.
Old things have passed away.
My past doesn't define me.
I like me.
In fact, I love me.
And I forgive me.

#SpeakLife: Day 71

Day 72

Matthew 18:20
"For where two or three are gathered in my name, there am I among them."

Reflection:
Families have to stay prayed up, and don't overlook the power of praying together. Make this a routine, a bonding experience. This is a great way to start your day. Families stay prayed up! You have to be mentally ready for the enemy. He comes to kill, steal, and destroy.

Goal:
On this morning, before you leave the house, pray over your family.

Repent and pray for:
- Protection
- Wisdom
- Guidance
- Divine Favor
- Healing

#SpeakLife: Day 72

Day 73

Matthew 10:30
But even the hairs of your head are all numbered.

✳

Reflection:
You're not supposed to fit in. Stop trying! You're different! You can't hide it. People will drop off and the right people will be added. It's okay to be different!

Goal:
Now, with your head held high, declare that even if no one else does, you like you.

Identify one way in which you can help a young girl embraces her differences and love herself.

#SpeakLife: Day 73

Day 74

1 Thessalonians 5:11
Therefore encourage one another and build one another up, just as you are doing.

Reflection:
Your later is greater! Let the past go! I don't care if it happened yesterday! It's still the past. Get up, dust off, and take another step. Before you know it, you're walking without stumbling for one day. Then one day turns into one week; one week will be one month; one month will be one year. And guess what? You might fall again. So freaking what? Get up, dust off, and take another step! Never give up on you!

Goal:
What part of your past continues to haunt you? It's okay not to forget, but have you forgiven?

Whether it was an old lover, an abuser, or yourself, it's critical that you dust yourself off and keep moving.

Find one person in your life to be your accountability partner. On schedule (daily, weekly, or monthly), you'll check in to encourage one another and build one another up.

#SpeakLife: Day 74

Day 75

ROMANS 8:28
And we know that for those who love God all things work together for good, for those who are called according to his purpose.

REFLECTION:
Don't be fooled. There is a blessing in long suffering. When you come out of this, you will be bold as a lion. You will fear no evil. You will know that the Lord thy God is with you. You will know that He will never leave you nor forsake you! Troubles don't last always.

Weeping may endure for the night, but joy cometh in the morning.

GOAL:
REPEAT AFTER ME:
I have joy, unspeakable joy.
I have peace that passes all understanding.
The joy of the Lord is my strength.
I am blessed beyond measure.

I love with the love of the Lord and forgive like I want to be forgiven.

In Jesus' name, Amen!

#SpeakLife: Day 75

#SpeakLife into Your Career

※

God has a plan for you. Stop looking at your current situations and circumstances. He can use anything or anybody. He will get the glory. No matter how bad the story may seem. Believe it and receive it. It's going to be okay. If He brought you to it, He will bring you through it.

Oftentimes in our careers, we're told that it's not what you know, it's who you know. Well, guess what? You know Jesus! Not only do you know Him, but you are His child. You are the apple of His eye. You are wise, healthy, wealthy, far more than a conqueror, and more than enough.

Repeat after me:
I can and will because I believe in me, and I know that no weapons formed against me shall prosper. I am what I say I am. I bind confusion, strife, and jealousy. What God has for me, it is for me. I will keep my eyes on my own prize and I won't allow my past to define my future.

My future is called blessed.

In Jesus' name, Amen!

Day 76

Matthew 14:22-25

And straightway Jesus constrained his disciples to get into a ship, and to go before him unto the other side, while he sent the multitudes away. And when he had sent the multitudes away, he went up into a mountain apart to pray: and when the evening was come, he was there alone. But the ship was now in the midst of the sea, tossed with waves: for the wind was contrary. And in the fourth watch of the night Jesus went unto them, walking on the sea.

✷

Reflection:
I learned that when you're almost at the promise, that's when the devil starts telling more lies. In the story where Peter said to God, if it's you, Lord, let me walk to you on water. Peter started to walk on water, but took his eyes off God and started to sink. See, Peter allowed the devil to plant doubt into his mind. He was *almost* at the promise.

When it gets hard, pray harder, seek God harder; believe harder. Your praise should match your expectancy. God is rebuilding your structure on good ground so that He can add power. If you build a house and add power to it before it is ready, you will burn the house down. Fight with your faith to get through the journey to your destiny. It's your promise!

Goal:
Write a letter to yourself from the perspective of the 100-year-old woman inside of you. What advice would she have for where you are now in life and in your career?

#SpeakLife: Day 76

Day 77

2 Timothy 1:7
For God gave us a spirit not of fear but of power and love and self-control.

✼

Reflection:
Whenever you think you can't, open your mouth and say you can. The past can't hold you back. It can only throw you forward.

Goal:
Are you awaiting a promotion, raise or a new career path?

Oftentimes, when waiting to be blessed, we consider all the reasons why we shouldn't be. Even if you made a mistake on the job, the prize is still yours.

Right now, #SpeakLife against your doubt, confusion, and insecurities.

#SpeakLife: Day 77

Day 78

Philippians 4:13
I can do all things through Jesus Christ who strengthens me.

REFLECTION:
If YOU don't believe in YOU, how can YOU expect others to believe in YOU?

GOAL:
If you believed in you as much as God believed in you, what would you be doing differently?

How would you be living?

Reflect on why you aren't living this way already? What's holding you back?

For every excuse, write today's scripture next to it.

Now, keep repeating this to yourself until your mind, body and soul line up with the Word of God.

#SpeakLife: Day 78

Day 79

Deuteronomy 28:13
And the Lord will make you the head and not the tail; you shall be above only, and not be beneath, if you heed the commandments of the Lord your God, which I command you today, and are careful to observe them.

REFLECTION:
Today, expect a breakthrough. Dress for it! Speak it! Walk like it! Act like it! Now watch it manifest.

GOAL:
REPEAT AFTER ME:
I am successful and I am wise.
I am courageous.
I have victory.
I am enough.
No weapons that forms against me shall prosper.
I am a light in darkness.
My cup runs over with blessings.
Even though I'm going through the valley, I will fear no evil; for the Lord thy God is with me and He will see me through.

In Jesus' name, Amen!

#SpeakLife: Day 79

Day 80

1 Corinthian 3:16
Do you not know that you are God's temple and that God's Spirit dwells in you?

REFLECTION:
You have everything in you that you need. Anything else is a want. That's not to say that our desires are wrong, but that we have everything in us to obtain the things that we desire to have.

GOAL:
Make a list with two columns.

In one column, list your needs.

In the other, list your wants.

Knowing that you already have obtained everything that you need, write a plan to acquire the things that you want.

#SpeakLife: Day 80

Day 81

John 14:22
"Truly, truly, I say to you, whoever believes in me will also do the works that I do; and greater works than these will he do, because I am going to the Father."

Reflection:
He's working it out on your behalf. No matter what it looks like right now, just know your future is called blessed. Now walk in it!

Goal:
Repeat after me:
I am walking in expectation.
I expect a miracle
I expect the impossible.
I am blessed and rich.
I deserve to be happy because I am a child of the most high.
Weapons may form, but they will never prosper.

In Jesus' name, Amen!

#SpeakLife: Day 81

Day 82

Matthew 6: 25-27
"Therefore I tell you, do not worry about your life, what you will eat or drink; or about your body, what you will wear. Is not life more than food, and the body more than clothes? Look at the birds of the air; they do not sow or reap or store away in barns, and yet your heavenly Father feeds them. Are you not much more valuable than they? Can any one of you by worrying add a single hour to your life?

✵

Reflection:
Why are you worrying about your future and stressing about your past? STOP allowing the past to hold you hostage. STOP allowing the future to hold you in bondage. Either way, you're standing still, not moving or progressing. You have the power to succeed in life. All you have to do is believe it, speak it, and do it.

Goal:
Repeat after me:
I can do all things through Christ who gives me strength.
I am the head, not the tail.
I am not depressed, oppressed, or suppressed.
I have joy, unspeakable joy.
I have peace that passes all understanding.
I can move on after a bad relationship.
I can get over hurt and pain.
I can do all things.

In Jesus' name, Amen!

#SpeakLife: Day 82

Day 83

Joshua 1:9
Have I not commanded you? Be strong and courageous. Do not be frightened, and do not be dismayed, for the Lord your God is with you wherever you go.

※

Reflection:
This morning, I found myself thinking about way too much at once. I know that I'm not the only people that do this. It's called worrying. This verse reminds me that no matter what, I don't have to be frightened or dismayed. I only have to be strong and courageous. I don't have to worry about anything in neither my personal nor professional life.

Goal:
Repeat after me:
No weapons formed against me shall prosper.
I control my destiny with the words I say out of my mouth.
I have the power of life and death with my words.

I have the power to change my thoughts in order to change my life.

I will not worry nor fright.
I have everything in me to be successful!

In Jesus' name, Amen!

#SpeakLife: Day 83

Day 84

2 Timothy 1:7
For God did not give us a spirit of timidity, but a spirit of power, of love and of self-discipline.

Reflection:
Fear is ever-present. It's going to be there. Acknowledge it and move on. Once you begin to believe that you've mastered dodging fear, doubt shows up. Doubt is a product of fear. Being afraid doesn't knock your courage. It's how you react to it that matters most. Sometimes you got to get cocky on your fears and doubts and say, "I ain't never scared, NOW what?" Fight back with your faith, actions, and words! Your body will line up. I promise!

Goal:
What are your biggest fears? Be honest. Acknowledging them is the first step of conquering them.

What are your dreams and desires?

Did you know that on the other side of your fear is your dream?

#SpeakLife: Day 84

Day 85

Luke 10: 38-42

Now as they went on their way, Jesus entered a village. And a woman named Martha welcomed him into her house. And she had a sister called Mary, who sat at the Lord's feet and listened to his teaching. But Martha was distracted with much serving. And she went up to him and said, "Lord, do you not care that my sister has left me to serve alone? Tell her then to help me." But the Lord answered her, "Martha, Martha, you are anxious and troubled about many things, but one thing is necessary. Mary has chosen the good portion, which will not be taken away from her."

※

Reflection:
In putting forth our best efforts, it's so easy to get wrapped up in distractions. Stay focused. Keep your eye on the prize. And remember to only work on one task a time. Don't allow distractions to be your main attraction!

Goal:
If you have a to-do list, go get it. If not, make one.

Prioritize your list in order of greatest to least importance. Afterwards, make a note of common distractions for each task.

Now that you've acknowledged the distractions, be conscious of avoiding them.

Day 86

Isaiah 40: 31
But those who wait on the Lord shall renew their strength; they shall mount up with wings like eagles. They shall run and not be weary. They shall walk and not faint.

Reflection:
Whether you work for someone else or work for yourself, there comes a point where it seems too much. You'll be begin to feel outdone. Beat. A tense work environment will make this even worse, but I have good news. You shall run and not be weary. You shall walk and not faint.

Goal:
Knowing that you'll be okay, let's take this time to pray for those we work with.

Whoever comes to mind first obviously needs the prayer the most. Get emotional about it!

#SpeakLife: Day 86

Day 87

Psalm 138:8
The Lord will fulfill his purpose for me;
your steadfast love, O Lord, endures forever.
Do not forsake the work of your hands.

✳

REFLECTION:
When you realize what your purpose is, you will understand the journey. Initially, it may feel like chaos or disorganization. You may feel scatterbrained and unfocused. You could very well be finding yourself bumping into walls at every which way you turn. Be patient. Your victory is around the corner.

Oftentimes, when we think of our purpose, we think of a solo journey. Such belief can lead to your purpose feeling more like a burden. However, the scripture reads that God will fulfill his purpose for you. It goes on to warn you not to forsake the work of your hands. It's right there. Your job is to keep moving; keep spreading His word; keep fulfilling your passions. God is definitely going to fulfill His purpose for you.

GOAL:
On a post-it note or index card, write this scripture. Post it somewhere in your workspace.

When you're feeling confused or frustrated, it will serve as your reminder.

Day 88

Proverbs 28:13
Whoever conceals his transgressions will not prosper, but he who confesses and forsakes them will obtain mercy.

Reflection:
If you're not making mistakes, then you're not doing anything. I am positive that a doer makes mistakes. That's how we learn. Live. Learn. Love. Admitting to a mistake that you've made on the job can be one of the most difficult things to do.

Goal:
Make a promise to yourself that the next time you make a mistake—regardless of how big or small it is—you'll confess.

Speaking life is speaking truth.

Your confession will free you to own your humanity, free you from guilt, and free you to prosper.

#SpeakLife: Day 88

Day 89

Isaiah 55:11
So shall my word be that goes out from my mouth; it shall not return to me empty, but it shall accomplish that which I purpose, and shall succeed in the thing for which I sent it.

Reflection:
A personal confession is a declaration, a verbal stance. It has nothing to do with who you were, but who you are and the greater that you set out to achieve. They are life-changing keepsakes that shall not return to you empty!

Goal:
Write your own personal confession, including answers to the following questions:

- What do you think about yourself?
- What are you saying about yourself?

Afterwards, Repeat after me:
I am more than enough.
I will finish what I start.
I believe in me.
Everything I do will be successful.
My close friends are positive.
My family is healing.
I will love with the love of the Lord.
I will forgive like I want to be forgiven.

In Jesus' name, Amen!

#SpeakLife: Day 89

Day 90

Proverbs 18:16
A man's gift makes room for him,
And brings him before great men.

Reflection:
Choosing between business and pleasure isn't an issue when your business is your pleasure. When you're fulfilling your purpose, your gift, you're blessed with endless opportunities and more balance. The problem, however, is that we oftentimes get stuck in careers that have nothing to do with what we are passionate about.

Goal:
Are you passionate about your career? Does it enable you to use your God-given gift? If so, take a moment to breathe the beauty of that in.

It's so easy to get distracted from our purpose in the name of a dollar. Describe how you know when you've strayed off course.

On the other hand, if you are not passionate about your career, plan an escape route. What do you need to do to get where you need to be?

#SpeakLife: Day 90

Day 91

Habakkuk 2:2
Then the LORD replied: "Write down the revelation and make it plain on tablets so that a herald may run with it."

Reflection:
Stop looking for happiness in others and find it in yourself!

Goal:
Name some goals you have achieved.

How does it make you feel when you see your goals listed?

Are you writing goals daily?

#SpeakLife: Day 91

Day 92

MATTHEW 5:16
In the same way, let your light shine before others, so that they may see your good works and give glory to your Father who is in Heaven.

✸

REFLECTION:
Hey, you are going through to get others through. Believe it or not, *it's not about you*. Keep your eyes on the prize. Don't look to your left or to your right. Stay on *your* journey. It will lead you to your destiny. Trust God!

GOAL:
Who and what gets the bulk of your time and attention?

Is this in alignment with your purpose?

If not, how can you turn this around?

#SpeakLife: Day 92

Day 93

1 Chronicles 29:17-18

I know, my God, that you test the heart and have pleasure in uprightness. In the uprightness of my heart I have freely offered all these things, and now I have seen your people, who are present here, offering freely and joyously to you. O Lord, the God of Abraham, Isaac, and Israel, our fathers, keep forever such purposes and thoughts in the hearts of your people, and direct their hearts toward you.

�֎

Reflection:
Do you have a Wait problem? Yeah, you heard me—a *Wait* problem. Waiting on something or someone to make you happy or successful. Get off your tail and exercise your faith and find your joy and take a leap of faith.

Goal:
Have you been waiting on others to approve your purpose? If so, why? Write about it.

When did this need for approval begin?

What steps can you take to change your mindset and build the courage to take that leap of faith?

#SpeakLife: Day 93

Day 94

JAMES 2:26
*For as the body without the spirit is dead,
so faith without works is dead also.*

✶

REFLECTION:
Finish what you've started. Get up and walk towards your victory. Remember, if God will bring you to it, He will also get you through it. Open your mouth and #SpeakLife, and then execute.

GOAL:
Where do you want to be exactly one year from today?

Where do you want to be living?

What do you want to be doing?

What will you have that you don't have now?

Write your desires, and then create a practical plan to achieving them. Dare to dream! I double dare you.

#SpeakLife: Day 94

Day 95

Matthew 20:16
So the last shall be first, and the first last:
for many be called, but few chosen.

※

Reflection:
Don't sleep on the last. They shall be the first. Wake up!

Goal:
What area of your career do you feel like the last?

Knowing that all things are possible through Christ and that you were created to be the head, #SpeakLife into those insecure areas. Know that you'll soon be first.

Make a list of ways that you can begin to prepare yourself for being first.

#SpeakLife: Day 95

Day 96

Matthew 14: 30-31
But when he saw the wind, he was afraid and, beginning to sink, cried out, "Lord, save me!" Immediately Jesus reached out his hand and caught him. "You of little faith," he said, "why did you doubt?"

✳

Reflection:
Never let your distractions be your main attraction. It was sent to paralyze you. Notice that when you take your eyes off Jesus, you start to sink like Peter. Jesus said walk on the water and don't look down. If you know this story you know that Peter stopped looking at Jesus and immediately began to sink in the water.

Goal:
Sometimes by reminding others of things, we also remind ourselves. So, send someone an e-mail, text message, or social media post, warning them of Peter's story.

Remind them to keep their eyes and energy forward lest they sink like Peter did.

#SpeakLife: Day 96

Day 97

Habakkuk 2:3
For still the vision awaits its appointed time; it hastens to the end—it will not lie. If it seems slow, wait for it; it will surely come; it will not delay.

※

Reflection:
Your God is big. So why is your vision so little? Get your mind right and focus.

Goal:
What is your vision for yourself?

Where are you professionally in the next five years?

Can this vision be made bigger? If so, dare to dream even bigger.

Get your mind right by aligning your vision with the power of God.

#SpeakLife: Day 97

Day 98

Matthew 6:31-34
So do not worry, saying, 'What shall we eat?' or 'What shall we drink?' or 'What shall we wear?' For the pagans run after all these things, and your heavenly Father knows that you need them. But seek first his kingdom and his righteousness, and all these things will be given to you as well. Therefore do not worry about tomorrow, for tomorrow will worry about itself. Each day has enough trouble of its own.

❋

Reflection:
Instead of worrying, practice speaking life.

Goal:
Even obsessively thinking of your next major move is a form of worrying.

What percentage of your thoughts is occupied with worry and need?

Grab a loose sheet of paper and scribble down every single thing that you've been finding yourself worrying about.

Afterwards, shred it, allowing your tendency to worry to be destroyed right along with the paper.

#SpeakLife: Day 98

Day 99

1 Peter 5:10
And after you have suffered a little while, the God of all grace, who has called you to his eternal glory in Christ, will himself restore, confirm, strengthen, and establish you.

Reflection:
Stop beating up on yourself. Stop allowing others to make you feel bad about that thing you struggle with. See, I am here to tell you that that thing you're struggling with is leading you straight to victory. Troubles don't last always. When you shake that thing off you, you will be restored. You will be walking in victory. You will be bold as a lion. You are going to beat it. I believe in you! Now believe in yourself! You go the victory; now walk in it!

Goal:
Repeat after me:
I am blessed.
I am walking towards my promise.
Weeping may endure for the night, but joy comes in the morning.

Troubles don't last always.
I am free from that thing.
No longer am I in bondage.

In Jesus' name, Amen!

#SpeakLife: Day 99

Day 100

Genesis 50:20
But as for you, you meant evil against me; but God meant it for good, in order to bring it about as it is this day, to save many people alive.

Reflection:
Healing starts on the inside. You feel it? It's called reconstruction... It doesn't feel good, but after the bleeding stops, the skin will grow a scab. It's going to itch. Don't scratch it or you're going to open the wound again. Make sure you put some protection on it. When it finishes healing, you will have new skin. It's for your good, so don't run away from it. It will make you stronger and wiser.

Goal:
What is your "it"? Whatever "it" is, it's guiding you to your purpose.

Thank it and keep moving forward. There is a blessing in reconstruction. It just depends on your focus.

Are you focusing on how the wound opened? Or, are you focusing on the healing?

Write about it.

#SpeakLife: Day 100

About La'Ticia Nicole

La'Ticia Nicole often says, *"I am just a girl from Detroit, MI who had dreams of success."* In 1992, she moved to North Carolina with $15, four outfits and a dream. The thought of being what others said she would become gave her the perseverance to gain admittance to Livingstone College in Salisbury, NC. Her passion for helping people led her to transfer to Winston Salem State University where she graduated with a Bachelor of Science in Nursing with honors.

La'Ticia Nicole furthered her education by receiving a Master of Business Administration from the University of Phoenix in Phoenix, Arizona. The two combined degrees allowed her to become an Executive Director in the long-term care industry thus accentuating her desire and passion for helping others. She credits her success to God, her mother, grandmother and a loving family who instilled strong morals, values and work ethics.

The term "entrepreneur" doesn't begin to describe who she is. She is a giver. Her strong desire to empower, promote self-awareness and self-esteem throughout the community lead her to create the nonprofit organization Professional Divas, Inc. To exemplify her passion for giving, the vision God gave her to feed 1,000 people during the 2013 Thanksgiving season was exceeded above and beyond when 2,500 people were fed nationwide.

Her public speaking platform, *La'Ticia Nicole #SpeakLife*, has allowed her to motivate others by simply speaking life into the dead areas that cause people to feel broken and angry. La'Ticia Nicole says, *"My foundation is based on the word of God; and, it has been my strength to move forward in continuing to #SpeakLife to as many people that will listen."*

La'Ticia Nicole Beatty is a child of God, wife, mother, daughter, sister, friend, mentor, philanthropist, sought-after motivational speaker, author and always a work in progress.

CONNECT WITH LA'TICIA OR SHARE YOUR FEEDBACK ON:

Amazon.com
Goodreads.com

@LaTiciaSpeaks   /LaTiciaNicole

THANK YOU FOR YOUR SUPPORT!

WWW.LATICIASPEAKLIFE.COM

YOUR WRITING IS A *Sacred* GIFT.

Your words are more than an unbound manuscript waiting to be released into the world. It's a soon-to-be executed *divine assignment,* which can only be delivered by you.

The way it looks, feels and impacts is a direct extension of who you were CREATED TO BE + DESIRE TO BECOME #TheGreatest

It's Time to Unleash Your Manuscript!

Are you ready? #PublishYourGift

CONNECT WITH US!
(866) 674-3340
Hello@PurposelyCreatedPG.com

www.PurposelyCreatedPG.com

Purposely Created
PUBLISHING GROUP